LETTER
TO A HINDU

A Letter
to a Hindu

THE SUBJECTION OF INDIA –
ITS CAUSE AND CURE

LEO TOLSTOY

With an introduction by
Mahatma Gandhi

RENARD PRESS

RENARD PRESS LTD

Kemp House
152–160 City Road
London EC1V 2NX
United Kingdom
info@renardpress.com
020 8050 2928

www.renardpress.com

A Letter to a Hindu first published in English in 1908
'Introduction' first published in 1909
This edition first published by Renard Press Ltd in 2020

Edited text © Renard Press Ltd, 2020
Extra Material © Renard Press Ltd, 2020

Cover design by Will Dady

Printed and hand-bound in the United Kingdom on Olin Smooth
(FSC certified) archival grade paper

ISBN: 978-1-913724-01-6

9 8 7 6 5 4 3 2 1

CONTENTS

CONTENTS

INTRODUCTION

THE LETTER PRINTED BELOW is a translation of Tolstoy's letter, written in Russian, in reply to one from the Editor of *Free Hindustan*. After having passed from hand to hand, this letter at last came into my possession through a friend who asked me, as one much interested in Tolstoy's writings, whether I thought it worth publishing. I at once replied in the affirmative, and told him I should translate it myself into Gujarati and induce others to translate and publish it in various Indian vernaculars.

The letter as received by me was a typewritten copy. It was therefore referred to the author, who confirmed it as his and kindly granted me permission to print it.*

To me, as a humble follower of that great teacher whom I have long looked upon as one of my guides, it is a matter of honour to be connected with the publication of his letter, such especially as the one which is now being given to the world.

It is a mere statement of fact to say that every Indian, whether he owns up to it or not, has national aspirations. But there are as many opinions as there are Indian nationalists as to the exact meaning of that aspiration, and more especially as to the methods to be used to attain the end.

One of the accepted and 'time-honoured' methods to attain the end is that of violence. The assassination of Sir Curzon Wylie* was an illustration of that method in its worst and most detestable form. Tolstoy's life has been devoted to replacing the method of violence for removing tyranny or securing reform by the method of non-resistance to evil. He would meet hatred expressed in violence by love expressed in self-suffering. He admits of no exception to whittle down this great and divine law of love. He applies it to all the problems that trouble mankind.

When a man like Tolstoy – one of the clearest thinkers in the western world, one of the greatest writers, one who as a soldier has known what violence is and what it can do – condemns Japan for having blindly followed the law of modern science, falsely so-called, and fears for that country 'the greatest calamities', it is for us to pause and consider whether, in our impatience of English rule, we do not want to replace one evil by another and a worse. India, which is the nursery of the great faiths of the world, will cease to be Nationalist India, whatever else she may become, when she goes through the process of civilisation in the shape of re-production on that sacred soil of gun factories and the hateful industrialism which has reduced the people of Europe to a state of slavery, and all but stifled among them the best instincts which are the heritage of the human family.

If we do not want the English in India we must pay the price. Tolstoy indicates it. 'Do not resist evil, but also do not yourselves participate in evil – in the violent deeds of the administration of the law courts, the collection of taxes and, what is more important, of the soldiers – and no one in the world will enslave you', passionately declares the sage

8

of Yasnaya Polyana. Who can question the truth of what he says in the following: 'A commercial company enslaved a nation comprising two hundred millions. Tell this to a man free from superstition and he will fail to grasp what these words mean. What does it mean that thirty thousand people, not athletes, but rather weak and ordinary people, have enslaved two hundred millions of vigorous, clever, capable, freedom-loving people? Do not the figures make it clear that not the English but the Indians have enslaved themselves?'

One need not accept all that Tolstoy says – some of his facts are not accurately stated – to realise the central truth of his indictment of the present system, which is to understand and act upon the irresistible power of the soul over the body, of love, which is an attribute of the soul, over the brute or body force generated by the stirring in us of evil passions.

There is no doubt that there is nothing new in what Tolstoy preaches. But his presentation of the old truth is refreshingly forceful. His logic is unassailable. And above all he endeavours to practise what he preaches. He preaches to convince. He is sincere and in earnest. He commands attention.

M.K. GANDHI
19th November, 1909

A LETTER
TO A HINDU

All that exists is One. People only call this One by different names.

THE VEDAS

God is love, and he that abideth in love abideth in God, and God abideth in him.

I JOHN IV 16

God is one whole; we are the parts.

EXPOSITION OF THE TEACHING OF
THE VEDAS BY VIVEKANANDA

I

Do not seek quiet and rest in those earthly realms where delusions and desires are engendered, for if thou dost, thou wilt be dragged through the rough wilderness of life, which is far from me.

Whenever thou feelest that thy feet are becoming entangled in the interlaced roots of life, know that thou has strayed from the path to which I beckon thee: for I have placed thee in broad, smooth paths, which are strewn with flowers. I have put a light before thee, which thou canst follow and thus run without stumbling.

KRISHNA*

I HAVE RECEIVED YOUR LETTER and two numbers of your periodical, both of which interest me extremely. The oppression of a majority by a minority, and the demoralisation inevitably resulting from it, is a phenomenon that has always occupied me, and has done so most particularly of late. I will try to explain to you what I think about that subject in general, and particularly about the cause from which the dreadful evils of which you write in your letter, and in the Hindu periodical you have sent me, have arisen and continue to arise.

The reason for the astonishing fact that a majority of working people submit to a handful of idlers who control their labour and their very lives is always and everywhere the same – whether the oppressors and oppressed are of one race, or whether, as in India and elsewhere, the oppressors are of a different nation.

This phenomenon seems particularly strange in India, for there more than two hundred million people, highly gifted both physically and mentally, find themselves in the power of a small group of people quite alien to them in thought, and immeasurably inferior to them in religious morality.

From your letter and the articles in *Free Hindustan*, as well as from the very interesting writings of the Hindu Swami Vivekananda* and others, it appears that, as is the case in our time with the ills of all nations, the reason lies in the lack of a reasonable religious teaching, which, by explaining the meaning of life, would supply a supreme law for the guidance of conduct and would replace the more-than-dubious precepts of pseudo-religion and pseudo-science with the immoral conclusions deduced from them and commonly called 'civilisation'.

Your letter, as well as the articles in *Free Hindustan* and Indian political literature generally, shows that most of the leaders of public opinion among your people no longer attach any significance to the religious teachings that were and are professed by the peoples of India, and recognise no possibility of freeing the people from the oppression they endure, except by adopting the irreligious and profoundly immoral social arrangements under which the English and other pseudo-Christian nations live today.

And yet the chief – if not the sole – cause of the enslavement of the Indian peoples by the English lies in this very absence of a religious consciousness and of the guidance for conduct which should flow from it – a lack common in our day to all nations East and West, from Japan to England and America alike.

II

O, ye who see perplexities over your heads, beneath your feet and to the right and left of you: you will be an eternal enigma unto yourselves until ye become humble and joyful as children. Then will ye find me, and, having found me in yourselves, you will rule over worlds, and looking out from the great world within to the little world without, you will bless everything that is, and find all is well with time and with you.

KRISHNA

TO MAKE MY THOUGHTS CLEAR to you I must go further back. We do not, cannot and, I venture to say, need not know how men lived millions of years ago, or even ten thousand years ago, but we do know positively that, as far back as we have any knowledge of mankind, it has always lived in special groups of families, tribes and nations in which the majority, in the conviction that it must be so, submissively and willingly bowed to the rule of one or more persons – that is, to a very small minority. Despite all varieties of circumstances and personalities, these relations manifested themselves among the various peoples of whose origin we have any knowledge; and the further back we go, the more absolutely necessary did this arrangement appear, both to the rulers and the ruled, to make it possible for people to live peacefully together.

So it was everywhere. But though this external form of life existed for centuries, and still exists, very early – thousands of years before our time – amid this life based on coercion, one and the same thought constantly emerged among different nations: namely that, in every individual, a spiritual element is manifested that gives life to all that exists, and that this spiritual element strives to unite with everything of a like nature to itself, and attains this aim through love. This thought appeared in most various forms at different times and places, with varying completeness and clarity. It found expression in Brahmanism, Judaism, Mazdaism (the teachings of Zoroaster), in Buddhism, Taoism, Confucianism and in the writings of the Greek and Roman sages, as well as in Christianity and Mohammedanism.* The mere fact that this thought has sprung up among different nations and at different times indicates that it is inherent in human nature and contains the truth. But this truth was made known to people who considered that a community could only be kept together if some of them restrained others, and so it appeared quite irreconcilable with the existing order of society. Moreover, it was at first expressed only fragmentarily, and so obscurely that, though people admitted its theoretic truth, they could not entirely accept it as guidance for their conduct. Then, too, the dissemination of the truth in a society based on coercion was always hindered in one and the same manner: namely, those in power, feeling that the recognition of this truth would undermine their position, consciously – or sometimes unconsciously – perverted it by explanations and additions quite foreign to it, and also opposed it by open violence. Thus the truth – that his life should be directed by the spiritual element which is its basis, which manifests itself as love and which is so natural to man – this truth, in order to force a way to man's consciousness, had to struggle not merely against the obscurity with which it was expressed and the intentional and unintentional distortions surrounding it, but also against deliberate violence, which, by means of persecutions and punishments, sought to compel men to accept religious laws authorised by the rulers and conflicting with the truth. Such a hindrance and misrepresentation of the truth – which had not yet achieved complete clarity – occurred everywhere: in Confucianism and Taoism, in Buddhism and in Christianity, in Mohammedanism and in your Brahmanism.

III

My hand has sowed love everywhere, giving unto all that will receive. Blessings are offered unto all my children, but many times in their blindness they fail to see them. How few there are who gather the gifts which lie in profusion at their feet; how many there are who in wilful waywardness turn their eyes away from them and complain with a wail that they have not that which I have given them; many of them defiantly repudiate not only my gifts, but me also – me, the Source of All Blessings and the Author of Their Being.

I tarry awhile from the turmoil and strife of the world. I will beautify and quicken thy life with love and with joy, for the light of the soul is love. Where love is, there is contentment and peace, and where there is contentment and peace, there am I, also, in their midst.

KRISHNA

The aim of the sinless One consists in acting without causing sorrow to others, although he could attain to great power by ignoring their feelings.

The aim of the sinless One lies in not doing evil unto those who have done evil unto him.

If a man causes suffering, even to those who hate him without any reason, he will ultimately have grief not to be overcome.

The punishment of evildoers consists in making them feel ashamed of themselves by doing them a great kindness.

21

*Of what use is superior knowledge in the One if he does not
endeavour to relieve his neighbour's want as much as his own?
If, in the morning, a man wishes to do evil unto another, in
the evening the evil will return to him.*

THE HINDU KURAL*

THUS IT WENT ON EVERYWHERE. The recognition that love represents the highest morality was nowhere denied or contradicted, but this truth was so interwoven everywhere with all kinds of falsehoods which distorted it that finally nothing of it remained but words. It was taught that this highest morality was only applicable to private life – for home use, as it were – but that in public life all forms of violence – such as imprisonment, executions and wars – might be used for the protection of the majority against a minority of evildoers, though such means were diametrically opposed to any vestige of love. And though common sense indicated that if some men claim to decide who is to be subjected to violence of all kinds for the benefit of others, these men to whom violence is applied may, in turn, arrive at a similar conclusion with regard to those who have employed violence to them, and though the great religious teachers of Brahmanism, Buddhism and, above all, of Christianity, foreseeing such a perversion of the law of love, have constantly drawn attention to the one invariable condition of love (namely, the enduring of injuries, insults and violence of all kinds without resisting evil by evil), people continued – regardless of all that leads man forward – to try to unite the incompatibles: the virtue of love, and what is opposed to love – namely the restraining of evil by violence.

PART III

And such a teaching, despite its inner contradiction, was so firmly established that the very people who recognise love as a virtue accept as lawful at the same time an order of life based on violence and allowing men not merely to torture but even to kill one another.

For a long time people lived in this obvious contradiction without noticing it. But a time arrived when this contradiction became more and more evident to thinkers of various nations. And the old and simple truth that it is natural for men to help and to love one another, but not to torture and to kill one another, became ever clearer, so that fewer and fewer people were able to believe the sophistries by which the distortion of the truth had been made so plausible.

In former times, the chief method of justifying the use of violence, and thereby infringing the law of love, was by claiming a divine right for the rulers: the tsars, sultans, rajahs, shahs and other heads of states. But the longer humanity lived, the weaker grew the belief in this peculiar, God-given right of the ruler. That belief withered in the same way and almost simultaneously in the Christian and the Brahman world, as well as in Buddhist and Confucian spheres, and in recent times it has so faded away as to prevail no longer against man's reasonable understanding and the true religious feeling. People saw more and more clearly, and now the majority see quite clearly, the senselessness and immorality of subordinating their wills to those of other people just like themselves, when they are bidden to do what is contrary not only to their interests but also to their moral sense. And so one might suppose that, having lost confidence in any religious authority for a belief in the divinity of potentates of various kinds, people would try to free themselves from subjection to it. But unfortunately not only were the rulers, who were considered supernatural beings, benefited by having the peoples in subjection, but as a result of the belief in, and during the rule of, these pseudo-divine beings, ever larger and larger circles of people grouped and established themselves around them, and under an appearance of governing took advantage of the people. And when the old deception of a supernatural and God-appointed authority had dwindled away, these men were only concerned to devise a new one which, like its predecessor, should make it possible to hold the people in bondage to a limited number of rulers.

IV

*Children, do you want to know by what your hearts should
be guided? Throw aside your longings and strivings after that
which is null and void; get rid of your erroneous thoughts about
happiness and wisdom, and your empty and insincere desires.
Dispense with these and you will know love.*

*Be not the destroyers of yourselves. Arise to your true being,
and then you will have nothing to fear.*

KRISHNA

NEW JUSTIFICATIONS HAVE NOW appeared in
place of the antiquated, obsolete, religious ones.
These new justifications are just as inadequate as
the old ones, but as they are new their futility cannot im-
mediately be recognised by the majority of men. Beside
this, those who enjoy power propagate these new sophistries
and support them so skilfully that they seem irrefutable,
even to many of those who suffer from the oppression these
theories seek to justify. These new justifications are termed
'scientific'. But by the term 'scientific' is understood just
what was formerly understood by the term 'religious': just
as formerly everything called 'religious' was held to be unquestionable simply because it was called religious, so now

all that is called 'scientific' is held to be unquestionable. In the present case the obsolete religious justification of violence which consisted in the recognition of the supernatural personality of the God-ordained ruler ('there is no power but of God') has been superseded by the 'scientific' justification which puts forward, first, the assertion that because the coercion of man by man has existed in all ages, it follows that such coercion must continue to exist. This assertion that people should continue to live as they have done throughout past ages – rather than as their reason and conscience indicate – is what 'science' calls 'the historic law'. A further 'scientific' justification lies in the statement that, as among plants and wild beasts there is a constant struggle for existence, which always results in the survival of the fittest, a similar struggle should be carried on among human beings – beings, that is, who are gifted with intelligence and love; faculties lacking in the creatures subject to the struggle for existence and survival of the fittest. Such is the second 'scientific' justification.

The third – most important, and unfortunately most widespread – justification is, at bottom, the age-old religious one, just a little altered: that in public life the suppression of some for the protection of the majority cannot be avoided – so that coercion is unavoidable, however desirable reliance on love alone might be in human intercourse. The only difference in this justification by pseudo-science consists in the fact that, to the question why such-and-such people and not others have the right to decide against whom violence may and must be used, pseudo-science now gives a different reply to that given by religion, which declared that the right to decide was valid because it was pronounced by persons possessed of divine power. 'Science' says that these decisions represent the will of the people, which under a constitutional form of government is supposed to find expression in all the decisions and actions of those who are at the helm at the moment.

Such are the scientific justifications of the principle of coercion. They are not merely weak, but absolutely invalid, yet they are so much needed by those who occupy privileged positions that they believe in them as blindly as they formerly believed in the immaculate conception, and propagate them just as confidently. And the unfortunate majority of men bound to toil is so dazzled by the pomp with which these 'scientific truths' are presented that under this new influence it accepts these scientific stupidities for holy truth, just as it formerly accepted the pseudo-religious justifications; and it continues to submit to the present holders of power, who are just as hard-hearted, but rather more numerous than before.

V

Who am I? I am that which thou hast searched for since thy baby eyes gazed wonderingly upon the world, whose horizon hides this real life from thee. I am that which in thy heart thou hast prayed for, demanded as thy birthright, although thou hast not known what it was. I am that which has lain in thy soul for hundreds and thousands of years. Sometimes I lay in thee grieving because thou didst not recognise me; sometimes I raised my head, opened my eyes and extended my arms, calling thee either tenderly and quietly or strenuously, demanding that thou shouldst rebel against the iron chains which bound thee to the earth.

KRISHNA

S O MATTERS WENT ON, AND STILL GO ON, in the Christian world. But we might have hope that in the immense Brahman, Buddhist and Confucian worlds this new scientific superstition would not establish itself, and that the Chinese, Japanese and Hindus, once their eyes were opened to the religious fraud justifying violence, would advance directly to a recognition of the law of love inherent in humanity and which had been so forcibly enunciated by the great Eastern teachers. But what has happened is that the scientific superstition

29

replacing the religious one has been accepted and secured a stronger and stronger hold in the East.

In your periodical you set out as the basic principle which should guide the actions of your people the maxim that: 'Resistance to aggression is not simply justifiable but imperative; non-resistance hurts both altruism and egotism.'*

Love is the only way to rescue humanity from all ills, and in it you too have the only method of saving your people from enslavement. In very ancient times love was proclaimed with special strength and clearness among your people to be the religious basis of human life. Love, and forcible resistance to evildoers, involve such a mutual contradiction as to destroy utterly the whole sense and meaning of the conception of love. And what follows? With a light heart and in the twentieth century you, an adherent of a religious people, deny their law, feeling convinced of your scientific enlightenment and your right to do so, and you repeat (do not take this amiss) the amazing stupidity indoctrinated in you by the advocates of the use of violence – the enemies of truth, the servants first of theology and then of science – your European teachers.

You say that the English have enslaved your people and hold them in subjection because the latter have not resisted resolutely enough and have not met force by force.

But the case is just the opposite. If the English have enslaved the people of India, it is just because the latter recognised, and still recognise, force as the fundamental principle of the social order. In accord with that principle they submitted to their little rajahs, and on their behalf struggled against one another, fought the Europeans, the English, and are now trying to fight with them again.

PART V

A commercial company enslaved a nation comprising two hundred millions. Tell this to a man free from superstition and he will fail to grasp what these words mean. What does it mean that thirty thousand men – not athletes, but rather weak and ordinary people – have subdued two hundred million vigorous, clever, capable and freedom-loving people? Do not the figures make it clear that it is not the English who have enslaved the Indians, but the Indians who have enslaved themselves?

When the Indians complain that the English have enslaved them it is as if drunkards complained that the spirit dealers who have settled among them have enslaved them. You tell them that they might give up drinking, but they reply that they are so accustomed to it that they cannot abstain, and that they must have alcohol to keep up their energy. Is it not the same thing with the millions of people who submit to thousands, or even to hundreds, of others – of their own or other nations?

If the people of India are enslaved by violence, it is only because they themselves live and have lived by violence, and do not recognise the eternal law of love inherent in humanity.

> *Pitiful and foolish is the man who seeks what he already has and does not know that he has it. Yes, pitiful and foolish is he who does not know the bliss of love which surrounds him and which I have given him.*
> KRISHNA

As soon as men live entirely in accord with the law of love, natural to their hearts and now revealed to them, which excludes all resistance by violence, and therefore hold aloof from all participation in violence – as soon as this happens, not only will hundreds be unable to enslave millions, but not even millions will be able to enslave a single individual. Do not resist the evildoer, and take no part in doing so, either in the violent deeds of the administration, in the law courts, the collection of taxes or, above all, in soldiering, and no one in the world will be able to enslave you.

VI

*O, ye who sit in bondage and continually seek and pant for free-
dom, seek only for love. Love is peace in itself, and peace which
gives complete satisfaction. I am the key that opens the portal
to the rarely discovered land where contentment alone is found.*

KRISHNA

W HAT IS NOW HAPPENING to the people of
the East as of the West is like what happens
to every individual when he passes from
childhood to adolescence and from youth to manhood. He
loses what had hitherto guided his life and lives without
direction, not having found a new standard suitable to his
age, and so he invents all sorts of occupations, cares, dis-
tractions and stupefactions to divert his attention from the
misery and senselessness of his life. Such a condition may
last a long time.

When an individual passes from one period of life to
another, a time comes when he cannot go on in senseless
activity and excitement as before, but has to understand
that, although he has outgrown what before used to dir-
ect him, this does not mean that he must live without any
reasonable guidance, but rather that he must formulate

for himself an understanding of life corresponding to his age, and, having elucidated it, must be guided by it. And in the same way, a similar time must come in the growth and development of humanity. I believe that such a time has now arrived – not in the sense that it has come in the year 1908, but that the inherent contradiction of human life has now reached an extreme degree of tension: on the one side, there is the consciousness of the beneficence of the law of love, and on the other the existing order of life which has for centuries occasioned an empty, anxious, restless and troubled mode of life, conflicting as it does with the law of love and built on the use of violence. This contradiction must be faced, and the solution will evidently not be favourable to the outlived law of violence, but to the truth which has dwelt in the hearts of men from remote antiquity: the truth that the law of love is in accord with the nature of man.

But men can only recognise this truth to its full extent when they have completely freed themselves from all religious and scientific superstitions and from all the consequent misrepresentations and sophistical distortions by which its recognition has been hindered for centuries.

To save a sinking ship, it is necessary to throw overboard the ballast, which, though it may once have been needed, would now cause the ship to sink. And so it is with the scientific superstition which hides the truth of their welfare from mankind. In order that men should embrace the truth – not in the vague way they did in childhood, nor in the one-sided and perverted way presented to them by their religious and scientific teachers, but embrace it as their highest law – the complete liberation of this truth from all and every superstition (both pseudo-religious and pseudo-scientific) by which it is still obscured is essential: not a partial, timid attempt, reckoning with traditions sanctified by age and with the habits of the people – not such as was effected in the religious sphere by Guru Nanak, the founder of the sect of the Sikhs, and in the Christian world by Luther,* and by similar reformers in other religions – but a fundamental cleansing of religious consciousness from all ancient religious and modern scientific superstitions.

If only people freed themselves from their beliefs in all kinds of Ormuzds, Brahmas, Sabbaoths and their incarnation as Krishnas* and Christs, from beliefs in paradises and hells, in reincarnations and resurrections, from belief in the interference of the gods in the external affairs of the universe and, above all, if they freed themselves from belief in the infallibility of all the various Vedas, Bibles, Gospels, Tripitakas, Korans and the like,* and also freed themselves from blind belief in a variety of scientific teachings about infinitely small atoms and molecules and in all the infinitely great and infinitely remote worlds, their movements and origin, as well as from faith in the infallibility of the scientific law to which humanity is at present subjected – the historic law, the economic laws, the law of struggle and survival, and so on – if people only freed themselves from this terrible accumulation of futile exercises of our lower capacities of mind and memory called the 'sciences',

and from the innumerable divisions of all sorts of histor-
ies, anthropologies, homiletics, bacteriologics, jurispru-
dences, cosmographies, strategies – their name is legion*
– and freed themselves from all this harmful, stupefying
ballast – the simple law of love, natural to man, accessible
to all and solving all questions and perplexities, would of
itself become clear and obligatory.

VII

Children, look at the flowers at your feet; do not trample upon
them. Look at the love in your midst and do not repudiate it.

KRISHNA

There is a higher reason which transcends all human minds.
It is far and near. It permeates all the worlds and at the same
time is infinitely higher than they.

A man who sees that all things are contained in the higher
spirit cannot treat any being with contempt.

For him to whom all spiritual beings are equal to the highest,
there can be no room for deception or grief.

Those who are ignorant and are devoted to the religious rites
only are in a deep gloom, but those who are given up to fruitless
meditations are in a still greater darkness.

UPANISHADS, FROM VEDAS

YES, IN OUR TIME ALL THESE THINGS must
be cleared away in order that mankind may
escape from self-inflicted calamities that have
reached an extreme intensity. Whether an Indian seeks
liberation from subjection to the English, or anyone else
struggles with an oppressor, either of his own nationality
or of another – whether it be a Negro defending him-

self against the North Americans, or Persians, Russians
or Turks against the Persian, Russian or Turkish govern-
ments, or any man seeking the greatest welfare for himself
and for everybody else – they do not need explanations
and justifications of old religious superstitions such as have
been formulated by your Vivekanandas, Baba Bharatis*
and others, or in the Christian world by a number of
similar interpreters and exponents of things that nobody
needs, nor the innumerable scientific theories about matters not only unnecessary but for the most part harmful.
(In the spiritual realm nothing is indifferent: what is not
useful is harmful.) What are wanted for the Indian as for
the Englishman, the Frenchman, the German and the
Russian are not constitutions and revolutions, nor all sorts
of conferences and congresses, nor the many ingenious
devices for submarine navigation and aerial navigation,
nor powerful explosives, nor all sorts of conveniences to
add to the enjoyment of the rich, ruling classes, nor new
schools and universities with innumerable faculties of
science, nor an augmentation of papers and books, nor
gramophones and cinematographs, nor those childish and
for the most part corrupt stupidities termed art – but one
thing only is needful: the knowledge of the simple and
clear truth which finds place in every soul that is not stu-
pefied by religious and scientific superstitions – the truth
that, for our life, one law is valid – the law of love, which
brings the highest happiness to every individual, as well
as to all mankind. Free your minds from those overgrown,
mountainous imbecilities which hinder your recognition
of it, and at once the truth will emerge from amid the
pseudo-religious nonsense that has been smothering it:

38

the indubitable, eternal truth inherent in man, which is one and the same in all the great religions of the world. It will, in due time, emerge and make its way to general recognition, and the nonsense that has obscured it will disappear of itself, and with it will go the evil from which humanity now suffers.

> *Children, look upwards with your beclouded eyes, and a world full of joy and love will disclose itself to you, a rational world made by my wisdom, the only real world. Then you will know what love has done with you, what love has bestowed upon you, what love demands from you.*
>
> KRISHNA

LEO TOLSTOY
Yasnaya Polyana
14th December, 1908

NOTE ON THE TEXT

On the 14th of December 1908 Leo Tolstoy wrote *A Letter to a Hindu* (in Russian) to Tarak Nath Das, and it was published in the latter's English-language journal, the *Free Hindustan*. When it came to the attention of Mahatma Gandhi, he wrote to Tolstoy on the 1st of October 1909 and asked his permission to print the letter in his South African newspaper, *Indian Opinion*.

'We have, however, not been able to secure the original,' Ghandi wrote, 'and we do not feel justified in printing it unless we are sure of the accuracy of the copy.'

To this, Tolstoy replied, six days later, '[I] am very pleased to have it translated into English,' although the translator's name was never given enough prominence to survive the years. This original translation is considered the authoritative text, and so it is upon this that the text of the Renard Press edition is based.

Gandhi's introduction is taken from the first edition of the first book-form publication (1909) of the letter.

In some instances, spelling, punctuation and grammar have been silently corrected to make the text more appealing to the modern reader.

NOTES

7   *It was… permission to print it*: See the Note on the Text.

8   *The assassination of Sir Curzon Wylie*: William Hutt Curzon Wyllie (1848–1909), assistant to the Secretary of State for India, was assassinated by Madan Lal Dhingra (1883–1909), who claimed that the murder was retaliation and revenge for 'inhumane British rule'.

15   KRISHNA: *Krishna: The Lord of Love* (1904) by Baba Premanand Bharati.

16   *Hindu Swami Vivekananda*: Swami Vivekananda (1863–1902) was an Indian spiritual leader whose teachings – based on those of Ramakrishna (1836–86) – considered all religions to be equal.

18   *Brahmanism… Mohammedanism*: Brahmanism was an early form of Hinduism, and is sometimes incorrectly used to refer to modern Hinduism; Mazdaism is another name for Zoroastrianism; Mohammedanism is an archaic term for Islam.

22   *The Hindu Kural*: The *Tirukkural* is a Tamil book of moral teachings.

30   *In your periodical… egotism*: The *Free Hindustan* was quoting the English philosopher Herbert Spencer (1820–1903), an early proponent of Darwinism who coined the term 'survival of the fittest'.

35   *Guru Nanak*: References to Guru Nanak (1469–1539), the founder of Sikhism, and Martin Luther (1483–1546), a German theologian and a principal figure in the German Protestant Reformation.

35   *Ormuzds… as Krishnas*: 'Ormuzd', a variant spelling of Ahura Mazda, is the chief deity in Zoroastrianism; the Lord 'Sabbaoth' is from Hebrew, usually translated as 'the Lord of Hosts'; in Hinduism, Krishna is an incarnation of the god Vishnu.

35   *Vedas… and the like*: Various religions' sacred texts: the Hindu Vedas, Buddhism's Tripitaka and the Islamic Koran.

36   *their name is legion*: 'Legion' here means 'great in number'.

38   *Baba Bharatis*: See note to p. 15.

EXTRA MATERIAL

A Brief Introduction to
Leo Tolstoy

Born on the 9th of September 1828 into a family of Russian nobility, Count Lev Nikolayevich Tolstoy is one of the highest-regarded writers of all time. His bibliography is vast, and many of his works run to huge extents – particularly his well-read novels; he is also known for his plays, short stories, essays and literary correspondence with notable figures.

Tolstoy's personal life is often skated around, in part due to his difficult relationship with his wife, Sofia, who was required to act as his secretary, scribe, business manager and spouse, while Tolstoy dedicated his life to writing. Nonetheless, they had thirteen children, eight of whom survived into adulthood.

In the 1870s Tolstoy went through a religious awakening, and he dedicated many works to the subject from then on, coming to influence pacifists with his writings – in particular, his 1894 philosophical treatise, *The Kingdom of God Is Within You*, is often cited as being of huge import in framing and influencing the views of Mahatma Gandhi and Martin Luther King Jr.

He is perhaps best known today for his novels *War and Peace* (1869) and *Anna Karenina* (1877), both of which have seen countless adaptations and editions over the years.

A Wider View
of the Conversation

Tarak Nath Das (1884–1958) was born into a lower-middle-class family in West Bengal. Impressing his headmaster and family at an early age with his talent with a pen, he was able to secure a university education at a Christian college in Kolkata. Soon after his degree, he embarked on a lecture tour in Madras, where he amassed a wide following. In the face of persecution by the Government due to his anti-British-rule stance, he fled to Japan, and from there on to Canada, where he started the *Free Hindustan*. In total, he lived forty-six years in exile, only returning to India in 1952 as a visiting professor.

Aware of Tolstoy's support of non-violent protest and aversion to oppression, Tarak wrote to the Russian author to solicit his support. Dated the 14th of December 1908, *A Letter to a Hindu* was the reply he received, which argued that the Indian people should seek to free themselves from British rule through non-violent protests and strikes and other forms of peaceful resistance.

The letter soon gained international attention after it was published, and it was passed to the young Mahatma Gandhi: 'A copy of your letter addressed to a Hindu [...] has been placed in my hands by a friend,' he wrote to Tolstoy, and went on to ask permission to print it in English in his South African newspaper, *Indian Opinion*, and, further, to have it translated into various Indian dialects (Gandhi himself would translate it into Gujarati).

Drawing on a variety of sources, cultures and teachings, Tolstoy's letter was instrumental in forming Gandhi's views on non-violent resistance – as Gandhi himself acknowledges in his introduction: 'To me, as a humble follower of that great teacher whom I have long looked upon as one of my guides, it is a matter of honour to be connected with the publication of his letter'.

The sources from which Tolstoy quotes are of importance themselves, and the epigraphs at the beginning of each part of the letter made as big an impression on Gandhi as the letter itself. The letter was responsible, for example, for introducing Gandhi to the *Tirukkural* ('*Sacred Verses*') – a book Tolstoy refers to as 'The Hindu Kural' – which is a collection of aphorisms on virtue, wealth and love. Gandhi went on to study the *Tirukkural* in depth, referring to it as 'a textbook of indispensable authority on moral life'.

Tolstoy's letter helped to form Gandhi's opinion on non-violent resistance, and it started a deep friendship between the two; they wrote to another a great many times after this, discussing the plight of Indians at the hands of the Government in both India and South Africa, as well as philosophical and literary matters.

In 1910, the year Tolstoy died, Herman Kallenbach (1871–1945), a wealthy landowner in South Africa, leant a 1,100 acre plot of land to Gandhi and around seventy of his followers for use as an ashram. Gandhi and his followers, '*styagrahis*', set up a self-sufficient farm, living area and school, which they called Tolstoy Farm out of respect for the Russian master whose philosophy they dedicated their lives to following.

OTHER CLASSIC NON-FICTION FROM
RENARD PRESS

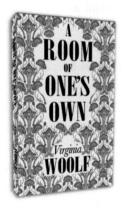

ISBN: 9781913724009
160pp • Paperback • £7.99

ISBN: 9781913724146
128pp • Paperback • £8.99

ISBN: 9781913724047
64pp • Pamphlet • £6.99

DISCOVER THE FULL COLLECTION AT
WWW.RENARDPRESS.COM